NLP in the Digital Age

Rewiring the Cybernetic Mind

Rex Morton

Copyright Page

Disclaimer

This book is intended to provide information about the fields of Neuro-Linguistic Programming (NLP) and Cognitive Behavioural Therapy (CBT) and their potential integration. While the author has made every effort to ensure that the information was correct at the time of publication, the author does not assume and hereby disclaims any liability to any party for any loss, damage, or disruption caused by errors or omissions, whether such errors or omissions result from negligence, accident, or any other cause.

The contents of this book should not be used as a substitute for professional advice, diagnosis, or treatment. The reader should always consult a qualified healthcare provider about mental health concerns or conditions. Never disregard professional psychological or medical advice or delay in seeking it because of something you have read in this book.

The views expressed in this work are solely those of the author and do not necessarily reflect the views of the publisher, and the publisher hereby disclaims any responsibility for them.

Including websites, links, or references to other resources does not mean that the author or the publisher endorses the information the organization or website may provide or its recommendations. Furthermore, the author does not guarantee the accuracy of these resources' information.

The use of any information provided in this book is solely at your own risk.

Introduction

Welcome to the World of NLP

Imagine you have a toolbox. In this toolbox, you have various tools that help you understand and influence the way people think and communicate. This toolbox is what we call Neuro-Linguistic Programming, or NLP for short. NLP is like a user manual for the mind, offering techniques and insights that help us understand how language affects our thoughts and behaviors.

The Birth of NLP

NLP started in the 1970s as a way to model excellence. It was like a recipe book for success, capturing the essence of how successful people communicate and think. Over time, it evolved from simple modeling techniques to a broad range of tools used in therapy, coaching, and personal development. It's like learning the language of your mind and using it to your advantage.

Enter the Digital Age

Fast forward to today, and we're living in the digital age. This era is marked by rapid technological advancements, especially in how we communicate. With the advent of the internet, smartphones, and social media, our ways of interacting have transformed dramatically. We're no longer just talking face-to-face; we're texting, emailing, and posting online.

How the Digital Age Changed Us

This digital revolution has not only changed how we communicate but also how we think and process information. Our brains are adapting to a world where information is abundant and attention is scarce. We're learning to filter, process, and respond to information in ways our ancestors never imagined.

The Impact on NLP

This shift to digital communication poses new challenges and opportunities for NLP. The principles of NLP, which were once applied in person, now need to be adapted for a world where conversations often happen through a screen. We're exploring how to build rapport, influence, and effectively communicate in a digital context. It's like learning a new dialect of the same language.

Why This Matters

Understanding NLP in the context of the digital age is crucial. It's not just about keeping up with the times; it's about harnessing the power of language and thought in a world where the rules of engagement are constantly evolving. Whether you're a professional, a student, or just someone interested in personal development, grasping the essence of NLP in this new era can be a game-changer.

Our Journey Ahead

In this chapter, we'll explore the foundations of NLP and how they're being reshaped by the digital age. We'll look at how technology is influencing the way we think, communicate, and connect with others. This is not just a journey through a set of techniques; it's an exploration of how we can adapt and thrive in a rapidly changing world.

Chapter 1: Foundations of NLP

The Story of NLP: From Past to Present

Let's start our journey by traveling back in time to the 1970s. Picture a world where the fields of psychology, linguistics, and computer science are blossoming. This is where NLP, or Neuro-Linguistic Programming, begins. It was born from the curiosity of understanding how successful people achieve their success. Think of it as trying to decode the secret recipe of excellence.

What Exactly is NLP?

Neuro-Linguistic Programming might sound like a complex term, but it's actually quite straightforward. "Neuro" refers to our mind and how we think. "Linguistic" is about language and how we use it. "Programming" is about our patterns of behavior and thought. Put simply, NLP is about understanding how we use our mind and language to create our reality and behaviors.

The Core Principles of NLP

NLP is based on a few key ideas:

The Map is Not the Territory: This means that how we perceive the world isn't the complete picture, just our personal interpretation of it.

There is a Structure to Experience: Our thoughts, feelings, and actions have a pattern, and if we understand this pattern, we can change it.

The Power of Flexibility: Being able to change our thinking and behavior makes us more effective in achieving our goals.

Tools and Techniques of NLP

Imagine having a toolkit that helps you improve how you communicate, think, and behave. That's what NLP techniques are like. Some popular tools include:

Rapport Building: Learning how to connect with others effectively.

Anchoring: Creating a trigger that brings about a desired feeling or state.

Reframing: Changing how we perceive a situation to alter its meaning and impact.

NLP in Action: Traditional Applications

NLP isn't just theory; it's practical and versatile. Here are some ways it's traditionally used:

In Therapy: Therapists use NLP to help people change unhelpful patterns of thinking and behavior.

In Coaching: Coaches use NLP to help individuals reach their personal and professional goals.

For Personal Development: Many people use NLP techniques for self-improvement, like boosting confidence or overcoming fears.

This chapter is your foundation in understanding NLP. We've explored its history, core principles, key techniques, and traditional applications. Remember, NLP is like a guide to better understand and influence our internal world and our interactions with others. As we move forward, keep these basics in mind, and you'll see how NLP can be a powerful tool in your life. Let's continue this journey together, unlocking the potential of our minds and words!

Chapter 2: The Digital Revolution

A New Era of Communication

Imagine waking up one day to find that the world communicates in a completely new way. That's what the digital revolution has done to us. It started with the rise of the internet, which brought us closer than ever before. Then came social media, smartphones, and various digital platforms, turning the world into a global village. Suddenly, we're not just talking to our neighbors; we're chatting with someone across the globe with just a few taps on a screen.

Transforming How We Interact

This shift to digital platforms has changed the very fabric of human interaction. We've gone from face-to-face conversations to emojis, texts, and video calls. It's not just about words anymore; it's about the speed, convenience, and new forms of expression. Imagine expressing joy not just with a smile but with a smiling emoji, a GIF, or even a meme. That's the new language of the digital age.

The Influence on Language

The digital world hasn't just changed how we talk; it's also transformed the language itself. Abbreviations like 'LOL' (laugh out loud) or 'BRB' (be right back) have become part of our everyday vocabulary. We're communicating faster, often in shorter forms, and sometimes entirely through symbols and images. It's like learning a new dialect of our own language, tailored for the digital landscape.

Enter Artificial Intelligence (AI)

In the midst of this communication evolution, there's a new player: Artificial Intelligence, or AI. It's like having a smart assistant that learns and adapts. AI is everywhere – from the suggestions you see on your online shopping site to the voice that answers when you ask your phone a question.

Machine Learning: AI's Learning Process

Machine Learning, a part of AI, is like teaching a computer to learn from experience. Just like you learn to recognize a cat by seeing many pictures of cats, machine learning algorithms learn from data to make decisions and predictions. It's how your email filters out spam or how your photo app recognizes your friends' faces.

Stepping into Virtual Reality (VR)

Virtual Reality (VR) is another marvel of the digital age. It's like stepping into a different world just by putting on a headset. In VR, you can tour a museum on the other side of the world, play a game as if you're really inside it, or even learn a new skill in a simulated environment.

In this chapter, we've journeyed through the exciting landscape of the digital revolution. From the rise of digital communication platforms to the wonders of AI and VR, it's clear that technology is reshaping our world in profound ways. As we embrace these changes, let's stay curious and open-minded, ready to explore all the possibilities this digital age has to offer. Let's move forward, together, into this brave new world of endless possibilities!

Chapter 3: NLP Meets Digital Communication

A New Playground for NLP

Imagine taking the timeless principles of NLP and mixing them with the fast-paced world of digital communication. That's what this chapter is all about. In a world where tweets, posts, and emails are the norm, how do we adapt NLP techniques to stay connected and influential?

Adapting NLP for the Digital World

Traditionally, NLP is about face-to-face interaction. But what happens when we remove the physical presence? It's like playing the same game with a new set of rules. In the digital realm, we rely more on written words and less on body language. So, we need to be more mindful of our word choices, tone, and even the timing of our messages.

Building Connections Online

Building rapport, which means creating a connection or understanding with someone, is a key part of NLP. In the digital world, this involves being empathetic and attentive in our online interactions. It's about crafting our messages in a way that resonates with our audience, whether it's through a thoughtful email, an engaging social media post, or even a well-timed text message.

Influencing Through Digital Channels

Influence in the digital world is about more than just convincing someone; it's about engaging and inspiring them. This could be through compelling storytelling on a blog, creating relatable content on social media, or simply being genuine and consistent in your online persona.

Hypothetical Case Studies: NLP in the Digital Age

Let's explore some examples:

Digital Marketing: Imagine a marketing campaign that uses language patterns to create a sense of urgency or desirability for a product. By understanding the customer's mindset, marketers can craft messages that are more likely to lead to a sale.

Social Media Influence: Consider a social media influencer who uses specific language patterns to build a loyal following. They might share stories that evoke emotions, use persuasive language, or interact with their audience in a way that fosters a sense of community.

In this chapter, we've delved into how NLP adapts and thrives in the digital landscape. By understanding and applying NLP techniques in our online interactions, we can build stronger connections, influence positively, and navigate the digital world more effectively. As we continue to blend the art of NLP with digital communication, let's embrace the power it brings to connect and influence across the digital divide. Let's keep learning and growing in this exciting digital era!

Chapter 4: NLP and Artificial Intelligence

A Meeting of Two Worlds

In this chapter, we explore the fascinating intersection of NLP (Neuro-Linguistic Programming) and AI (Artificial Intelligence). It's like bringing together the understanding of human communication from NLP with the computational power of AI. This synergy is opening up new possibilities and transforming how we interact with technology.

NLP Techniques in the Realm of AI

Imagine teaching a computer to understand and use human language in a way that seems almost natural. This is what happens when NLP techniques are integrated into AI. It's about programming computers to recognize patterns in language, understand context, and even interpret emotions, much like how we do it in human conversations.

Understanding Speech Recognition and Chatbots

One of the most common applications of this blend is in speech recognition and chatbots. Speech recognition is like teaching a machine to listen and understand what we say, turning spoken words into digital data. Chatbots, on the other hand, are like digital conversationalists. They use NLP to understand and respond to text inputs, providing assistance, information, or even company.

Natural Language Processing: AI's Language Skill

Natural Language Processing, or NLP (not to be confused with Neuro-Linguistic Programming), is a branch of AI that deals with the interaction between computers and human language. It's about enabling machines to read, decipher, and understand human languages in a valuable way. This technology powers everything from your smartphone's voice assistant to the customer service chatbot on your favorite shopping website.

Navigating the Ethical Landscape

As we merge NLP with AI, we also encounter ethical considerations. How do we ensure that these AI-driven applications are used responsibly? Issues like privacy, data security, and the potential for manipulation are important to address. It's about finding a balance between leveraging this technology for good and safeguarding against its misuse.

In this chapter, we've journeyed through the exciting world where NLP meets AI. We've seen how the principles of human communication are being translated into the language of machines, creating more intuitive, helpful, and engaging technologies. As we continue to advance in this field, it's crucial to keep the ethical considerations in mind, ensuring that the fusion of NLP and AI benefits us all. Let's embrace this new era of intelligent communication with optimism and responsibility!

Chapter 5: Virtual Reality and Experiential NLP

The Fusion of VR and NLP

Welcome to a chapter where reality meets virtuality. Here, we explore how Virtual Reality (VR) – a technology that lets you experience a computer-generated world as if it were real – is merging with NLP (Neuro-Linguistic Programming) to create transformative experiences. It's like putting on a headset and stepping into a world where you can not only see and hear but also feel and grow.

Immersive Learning with VR

Imagine learning new skills or working on personal development in a completely immersive environment. VR allows for this by creating realistic simulations. For instance, if someone wants to become more confident in public speaking, VR can simulate an audience, providing a safe space to practice and improve. The sensory-rich environment of VR makes learning more engaging and effective.

Therapy in Virtual Environments

VR is also revolutionizing therapy. It's like having a therapy session in a controlled, yet completely customizable, environment. People facing fears or phobias can be gently exposed to their fears in a virtual setting, allowing them to confront and work through their issues in a safe and controlled manner. This approach can be more flexible and less intimidating than traditional methods.

The Future of VR in Personal Development and Coaching

The potential of VR in personal development and coaching is vast. Imagine a future where coaches can create customized VR scenarios to help clients overcome personal challenges, build skills, or even explore different aspects of themselves. VR can offer a safe and controlled environment for deep self-exploration and targeted skill development, opening up new possibilities in personal growth.

In this chapter, we've seen how the combination of VR and NLP is creating new pathways for learning, therapy, and personal development. By stepping into virtual worlds, we can experience growth and transformation in ways that were once only imaginable. As VR technology continues to evolve, the prospects for its use in personal development and coaching are exciting and limitless. Let's keep our minds open to the endless possibilities that this blend of technology and personal growth techniques can bring.

Chapter 6: The Ethics of NLP in the Digital Age

The Ethical Landscape of Digital Communication

Welcome to a chapter where we explore the ethical side of using NLP (Neuro-Linguistic Programming) in our increasingly digital world. In this era of online communication, it's crucial to consider how we use words and technology responsibly. It's like having a powerful tool; we need to use it wisely and for the right purposes.

Persuasion vs. Manipulation

One of the key ethical concerns in using NLP digitally is the fine line between persuasion and manipulation. Persuasion is about influencing others positively, while manipulation involves using deceptive or unfair tactics. It's like guiding someone to a decision that benefits them (persuasion) versus leading them to a decision that benefits you at their expense (manipulation). We must always aim for the former, using our skills to empower and uplift, not exploit.

Privacy in the Digital World

With the use of NLP techniques in digital platforms, privacy concerns come to the forefront. When we communicate online, especially when using NLP methods, we often share and receive personal information. It's like entering someone's digital home; we need to be respectful and ensure that their information is kept secure and confidential.

Data Security in Digital NLP Applications

Another aspect of ethical concern is data security. In the digital age, information is a valuable commodity. When NLP applications collect data for personalization or analysis, it's vital to protect this data from misuse or unauthorized access. It's about building a digital environment where users can trust that their information is safe.

In this chapter, we've navigated through the ethical considerations of using NLP in the digital world. From ensuring the fine balance between persuasion and manipulation to safeguarding privacy and data security, it's clear that ethical practice is paramount. As we continue to use NLP and digital tools, let's commit to using them responsibly, always with respect and integrity. Let's create a digital space that is safe, respectful, and empowering for all.

Chapter 7: The Future of NLP

The Evolution of NLP and Technology

Imagine standing at the edge of a new frontier where the worlds of NLP (Neuro-Linguistic Programming) and technology are merging in exciting ways. As we look into the future, we see emerging trends where NLP is not just about human-to-human interaction but increasingly about human-to-machine communication. It's like learning a new language that helps us communicate with the digital world around us.

NLP Shaping the Digital Future

NLP is set to play a crucial role in shaping our digital future. As we interact more with AI and virtual platforms, NLP can make these interactions more natural and intuitive. It's like teaching machines to understand not just our words, but the intent and emotion behind them. This could lead to more empathetic AI, smarter chatbots, and digital assistants that understand us better.

Ready for an Interconnected, AI-Driven World

As we move towards a future where our lives are increasingly intertwined with AI and digital technologies, NLP will be key in ensuring these technologies are user-friendly and effective. It's about preparing ourselves to live and work in a world where AI is not just a tool, but a partner in our daily lives. This means not only understanding how to use these technologies but also how to interact with them effectively, ethically, and empathetically.

The Potential of NLP in Tomorrow's World

The potential for NLP in the future is vast. We could see enhanced learning environments powered by VR and NLP, AI-driven therapy and coaching that are more accessible and personalized, and even smarter home assistants that understand and anticipate our needs. It's a world where technology understands us better and works more seamlessly with us.

In this chapter, we've explored the exciting possibilities that lie ahead for NLP in an increasingly digital and AI-driven world. From enhancing our interactions with technology to shaping the very nature of these interactions, NLP is poised to play a pivotal role in our digital future. As we step into this future, let's embrace the opportunities and challenges it brings, ready to grow and adapt in this ever-evolving landscape. Let's journey forward with optimism and an open mind towards the endless possibilities that await!

Chapter 9: Conclusion

A Journey Through NLP and the Digital Age

As we reach the conclusion of our exploration into NLP (Neuro-Linguistic Programming) in the digital age, let's take a moment to reflect on the key insights and learnings from our journey. Think of this chapter as a map that highlights the paths we've traveled and the treasures we've discovered along the way.

Summarizing Our Discoveries

We began by understanding the foundations of NLP, discovering how it's like a toolbox for our minds, helping us understand and influence thoughts and behaviors.

We then navigated the digital revolution, seeing how technology has transformed the way we communicate and interact.

We explored the fusion of NLP with digital communication, learning how to adapt and thrive in online interactions.

The integration of NLP with Artificial Intelligence (AI) showed us a new frontier where human understanding meets machine intelligence.
We stepped into the immersive world of Virtual Reality (VR), witnessing how it can enhance learning and personal development.

The ethical considerations of using NLP and technology reminded us of the importance of responsible and respectful communication.

Looking into the future, we envisioned the evolving role of NLP in a world increasingly driven by interconnectivity and AI.

The Ongoing Relevance of NLP

In our fast-paced, ever-changing digital world, NLP remains more relevant than ever. It offers us a way to better understand ourselves and others, enhancing our communication in both the real and digital worlds. It's like having a compass that helps us navigate the complex landscape of human interaction, whether we're chatting online, working with AI, or engaging in personal development.

Embracing NLP for Positive Change

As we close this chapter, let's remember the power of NLP combined with technology for creating positive change. It's not just about what these tools can do; it's about how we use them. By using NLP and technology responsibly, we can create a world that's more connected, empathetic, and understanding.

We stand at the threshold of exciting possibilities, armed with the knowledge and insights from our exploration of NLP in the digital age. Let's move forward with a commitment to using these tools for the greater good, fostering positive change, and building a brighter, more connected future for everyone. Let's take these learnings and turn them into actions that make a real difference in our lives and the lives of those around us. The future is ours to shape, with the power of our words and the support of our digital tools.

About the Author

Rex Morton is a renowned author and researcher in the United Kingdom with a passionate interest in the human mind, specifically in Cognitive Behavioural Therapy (CBT) and Neuro-Linguistic Programming (NLP).

Morton has spent a considerable portion of his professional life diving deep into the theories and principles that form the backbone of these two compelling fields.

Although Morton does not have clinical experience, his intense curiosity and dedication to studying these subjects have made him a respected figure in the field. He has thoroughly researched the integration of NLP techniques into CBT, offering fresh perspectives and insights into how these two methodologies can complement each other to enhance understanding of human cognition and Behaviour.

As an author, Morton has successfully communicated his knowledge and passion to a broader audience, making complex psychological theories accessible to professionals and interested laypersons. His writing is characterized by a clear, engaging style and a focus on the practical application of theories, making them relevant to everyday life.

In his personal life, Morton is an ardent lover of the natural world, often spending his free time exploring the British countryside. His passion for landscape photography allows him to capture and share the beauty of these excursions. Despite his accomplishments, Morton is known for his humility and eagerness to continue learning. His work continues to inspire those interested in the intricate workings of the human mind and the exciting possibilities presented by the integration of NLP and CBT.

Stay Connected: Join the Journey at RexMorton.com

If you've found the content of this book enlightening and wish to continue your journey of understanding the human mind, I warmly invite you to visit my website at www.rexmorton.com. The website serves as a hub of knowledge where I share my latest findings, thoughts, and insights on NLP and related topics.

I also encourage you to subscribe to the newsletter available on the website. By subscribing, you'll receive regular updates on a range of topics, from detailed discussions on specific NLP techniques and their application in other fields to the latest research.

The newsletter is also the first place I'll share news of upcoming releases. Whether it's the announcement of a new book, the launch of an online course, newsletter subscribers will be the first to know. This is a great opportunity to continue learning directly from me, deepening your understanding of NLP and related topics, and enhancing your skills in applying these techniques in your own life or professional practice.

I'm looking forward to sharing this journey with you.